GOLF

FOR THE

Girls

TAKE THAT BOOKS

Golf for The Girls

Take That Books is an imprint of
Take That Ltd.
P.O.Box 200
Harrogate
HG1 4XB

Copyright © 1995 Alma Walker & Take That Ltd.

Compiled from a series of articles originally published in Golf Monthly.
Illustrated by Joe McKeough

10 9 8 7 6 5 4 3 2 1

ISBN 1-873668-11-2

Layout and typesetting by
Take That Ltd., P.O.Box 200, Harrogate, HG1 4XB.

Printed and bound in Great Britain.

Golf for The Girls

The Course

You've Taken Up The Game

Success and glory to all woman golfers!

You've Taken Up The Game

Although the physical differences between men and women may be a source of great pleasure in the proper place, there is one vast area of sexual combat where these basic and fundamental distinctions put the more fragile, tenderhearted and sensitive sex at a massive disadvantage. ***And that's the golf course.***

Even the most cursory glance along the bookshelf of any fullblooded member of the Men's Section will evince the millions of words printed about golf. Advice about the swing, the grip, the stance, the left arm theory and the right hand theory, addressing the ball, the position of the head, shoulders, hips, feet, and right eyebrow. Priceless advice from all the great players from Braid to Ballesteros. Advice which you would have to be as brainless as a brassie not to realise was written exclusively by men and for men.

Idly leafing through any of these books you will find the illustrations show only brawny muscled Apollos with thighs like pit props and arms like steel girders in positions which, if a woman tried to emulate, would give us an odds on chance of trapped nerves, twisted ankles, pulled ligaments, ruined hairdo's and broken wrists (not, I may add, "broken" as in golf!)

So who is to step forward as adviser to the liberated ladies of the links? Who indeed! It's about time somebody did. What percentage of golf coverage do the Ladies Tournaments have on T.V? If you blink you'll miss it.

But all is not lost.

Having been thrown out of more Golf Clubs than I care to mention, for things like Slowing Down Play, Using Bad Language in the Locker Room and Letting the Air out of the Lady Captain's tyres, I feel in a strong position to give advice.

We all, don't we, want to get our handicaps down to 33, even if only to boost our egos? And how shall we achieve this if nobody encourages and helps us? There are, of course, a few of us who actually do achieve being a 23 or (gosh!) an 18, but they are never well known for giving a helping hand or a kindly word to a 36-plus. All they do is reduce our knees to jelly if they so much as nod to us as they stride their spiked shoes past us in the Locker Room.

It is important, you must agree, in studying this Royal and Ancient Game, to get one's priorities right, so I shall call my first lesson: *What to Wear, or, to put a finer point on it, What Not To Wear for Golf.*

1

What *Not* To Wear for Golf

You may, like me, have realised the hard way that it is desirable and necessary to wear something that is fairly loose around the shoulders. A sexy shirt that slits from top to bottom when you raise your arms, or a stylish model that is a 12 when you are a 16 so that the buttons fly off when faced with any strain - such as breathing - may raise the blood pressure of (and thus give you an advantage over) a few elderly retired gentlemen, but it will not help you to concentrate on the game. And concentrate we must. As I shall tell you later.

Also, arriving in a purple silk cat suit and high heeled pink sandals, or hot pants with lurex socks, will do nothing towards getting you accepted into the sagging bosom of the Ladies Section. So realise from the word "Go" that you'll be infinitely more acceptable in a baggy tweed skirt and jersey (preferably home knitted) worn over a stoutly constructed bra. You'll be less of a threat.

Nails should be short and unpainted and, if you can bear to wear a hairnet, you'll be heading for the Big Time.

Shoes should look the part. Remember that much is expected from women who wear *white* golf shoes, so only buy these if you already have a glass fronted display cabinet full of silver trophies and unwrapped presentation golf balls. In the high-handicap class you must settle for brown or blue shoes, bearing in mind that spikes are impressive, even if they do make you totter down the fairways like a centipede in the wrong sized Wellingtons, while the sheer weight makes you fear for the future of your Metatarsal arches.

Very tight slacks that show a ridge where your knickers end, are also to be avoided (Remember the Retired Elderly Gents).

Golf for The Girls

"That's agreed then, all husbands are grounded until we've sorted her out"

Golf for The Girls

So, if you belong to a Club where it is "in" to wear trousers, be sure to choose pale pink, apple green or baby blue ones (washable Crimplene in good weather) several sizes too large. These must have copious pockets to hold tees, balls, pep pills, score card, pencils, bandaids, markers and a brandy flask (all of which you're never given time enough to return to your golf bag). The important thing to remember is that they must hang in folds all around the tum and bum, totally disguising the fact that underneath there might be a shape worthy of causing male members to take their eyes, albeit briefly, off the ball.

One does, of course, see odd things. Like a girl I once saw (and I swear this is the truth) having a lesson wearing a full length red chiffon dress and earrings like chandeliers. Some women get rather carried away by golf pros.

Dont' wear your best rings, for the simple reason that you won't get your golf glove over them. Buy some small, cheaper diamonds for golf, with low settings. Emeralds and sapphires are quite acceptable but, once again, watch when you buy them that they are set quite flat. It is a good idea to take a golf glove along to the jewellers with you, just to be on the safe side. You may, of course, take your best rings to the course, but lock these in the glove compartment of your car and just pop them on after the game for coffee with the girls.

Necklaces of the swinging medallion kind are not a good idea. It is difficult to really fix your eyes on the ball at address if there is a huge gold nugget on a chain oscillating between you and it. This, in fact, was once known to hypnotise one lady member who slid to the ground in a deep sleep before she had even started on her backswing.

If, like me, you are a failed member of several Golf Clubs and, also like me, are a sucker for those jerseys on sale in the pro shops with the Club's insignia emblazoned on the front, a most valuable tip is never to wear these jerseys at your new Club. Somehow, if you walk into the Change Room with a former and alien Club's name embroidered across your boobs the whole assembly will cleave together and ostracise you. One moment there will be lively talk about knock-outs and eclectics and isn't-it-shocking-about-poor-Muriel and then - suddenly - silence. And no matter how much you ache to know more about poor Muriel, you never will.

So, put aside an afternoon to go over all the badges on previous jerseys with a felt pen. Any good stationer has these - black for black jerseys, blue for blue jerseys, etc. etc. It seems a sad thing to have to cover all those lovely badges you had thought to impress people with but, believe me, it is good sound advice if you wish to be a warmly accepted member of the Ladies Section.

And don't be put off by those small sinister enamelled badges often seen pinned to the indefatigable bosoms of senior lady members. Underneath them could well beat kindly and sympathetic hearts. *'Honestly'*.

"No, sorry, this one will reflect too much sun"

2

Sticks and Things

It is all right to start off with what is called a "half set" of clubs - by which they mean even numbers or odd numbers only, but not the maximum tote load which I seem to remember someone once telling me must not exceed fourteen pieces. Of course, as your handicap goes down and your status goes up, having a half set is something to be ashamed of, like bad breath or underarm perspiration. But, for starters, a half set is fine. What beginner needs a full set anyway?

Most of your clubs, you will find, send the ball the same distance, whether it is called a seven or a two. It's just a snob thing really, all this lining up and saying "Do you think this is a five or a seven shot?" Once you do get into that frame of mind you're likely to spend most of your game dithering around in your golf bag making decisions. Usually quite erroneous ones. I've found it better just to grab one that looks more or less clean and have a bash. Occasionally you'll be surprised.

If you haven't yet decided whether or not to take up golf, but seek merely to experience what it feels like, you can drift along to a public course and sink several weeks' housekeeping money into paying green fees and hiring clubs and a trolley from the resident pro. But the clubs he'll lend you will bear little or no resemblance to the gleaming creatures he has for sale in graded rows.

The clubs he will hire you will be covered in rust, have grips that are unfurling down the shaft like limp leather flags, screws hanging from the faces of the woods like old decaying teeth and be a suitable size and weight for Superman. And the trolley will have wheels like those you always manage to find at the supermarket, in addition to which the strap which holds on your golf bag will, of course, be broken.

On the whole I recommend asking around amongst your nephews or grandchildren and their friends, where you may find one kind enough, or amused enough at the idea of you even trying, to lend you his clobber.

Golf for The Girls

Don't be intimidated by your opponent's equipment

Never play with red balls. As this is advice to ladies only I can say this with impunity. Red balls suggest that you play in snow which, as you will realise, can only be done by very fine lady golfers indeed. Red balls suggest that you consider the weather and select from a vast store suitable ones for the day's play, perhaps to match your golf hat or your socks instead of plunging your hand into your bag and having a go with anything you find there that is still more or less round. Red balls are the kiss of death to what you had hoped would be a lasting friendship through the years, formed on the links.

So, I repeat, *never* play with red balls.

A New Set

This heading might make you think of teeth, or something daring to do with your hair, but put all such thoughts behind you. What we have to deal with now is buying clubs. If you are seriously into this game you will soon become aware of the psychological disadvantage of carrying around a scruffy old set of clubs you found, one wet day, in the attic, and you'll find yourself overwhelmed by an almost sexual longing to hold in your hands something truly worthy of all the effort you are putting into being - A Golfer.

Much thought has to go into buying new clubs and initially the most serious involves how you will keep from your husband/lover/father how much you paid for them. Here I would suggest inventing a friend who has been laid low by an illness likely to keep her permanently off the golf course (don't let your imagination run riot too much with this in case of an unexpected rush of sympathy, and possible follow up). Perhaps you can say that, before being stretchered off to hospital, she pinned a note on the Clubhouse notice board bequeathing to you her new set of clubs. Something like that.

Practise some stories in your mind before going to sleep at night until you find the one you're most comfortable with. Don't lose any precious sleep over it - remember that men are a pretty gullible lot.

Golf for The Girls

Unless you have a close, warm relationship with your Club pro its recommended that, for this momentous occasion in your life, you consult the most senior guru at a specialist golf shop. These, I regret to say, are almost entirely men - men used to dealing with men and, therefore, as you step over the threshold, unlikely to leap to their feet to assist you as they've already categorised you as "six plastic tees and two nearly-new golf balls".

To gain an advantage here I have discovered the best ploy is to hang around and unfurl a wad of high denomination notes which you will have collected in readiness from the bank. These you count out quietly to yourself, occasionally glancing in his direction. You will find the result quite electrifying.

Now you have got his full attention and if he's worth his salt he'll have you in a back room in no time, assessing your swing and, by the time you come out, you'll be ready to put your life in his hands.

But this euphoria won't last. As you return to the main arena of the shop, and have taken in what you were too nervous to notice before - hundreds of sets of clubs of every colour, length and dimension, and become aware of his voice in your ear, murmuring "Now, what shafts do you fancy - graphite, ceramic, steel, carbon, boron or kevlar?" you will feel your eyes glaze over and a be aware of a hard knot forming in your stomach reminding you of bygone days when you picked up your pen to tackle the first question in an algebra exam.

And when, hours later, you leave the emporium with your ears still ringing with phrases like "extra low torque, high modulus, bubble levels, high tensile, and carbon compression" remember all that really matters is that you can look down on your new purchase with the adoring gaze of a mother with a new baby. They're a beautiful colour - you love them - and together you'll make a great team.

Pro Shops.

Male orientated pro shops often offer for sale tin gadgets with slots in them for pencil, card, balls, tees, markers and cigarette packets. These are for screwing, with wing nut provided, close to the handle of your golf trolley. They usually come in beguiling colours and, when studied, seem to offer blissful freedom from the unaccustomed jangling weight of golfers' essential accoutrements in the bulging pockets of our golf pants or jerseys (if we have pockets, that is).

Beware of such gadgets. Pause to consider for a moment: you never see a man's trolley with one of these screwed on to it, and you will have to ask yourself why.

When you try one out in the pro shop - which you will be encouraged to do - and load it up with all the stuff you're toting around with you, a great feeling of lightness and freedom will surge over you leaving you wondering how you ever managed without one. Once you hand over the purchase price and stride out on to the course, however, you will realise that this simple charming little gadget is yet another manifestation of the sinister cunning of the male inventor's mind.

On even the slightest gradient the weight of this innocent little helpmate is sufficient to pitch your trolley handle, once you let it go, down into the grass thereby spilling your clubs head first all around you like a burst bag of split peas. The constant retrieving of your clubs and slotting them back in their rightful places is tiring, irritating, vexing and - eventually - hysteria-making. All of the '-ings' we don't need whilst we're out there. So, no matter how much you may feel drawn to these brightly painted appendages when you see them arranged at woman's-eye-level in your pro shop, be warned and say a firm "*No!*"

And distrust any man who buys you one for a present.

When all else fails, have a lesson

Having a few lessons at the outset is a good idea but, here again, Why are nearly all golf pros male? Why not ladies to teach lady golfers? What do men know about the discomfort of wearing an A cup instead of a B cup, or how tight knicker elastic can affect the follow-through? Not to mention Bad Days. But I would stress here that "having a lesson" does not mean that some divine man will sidle up behind you and place his strong arms around your waist and his sexy hands over yours (see "Sex on the Golf Course" - to follow).

Not a bit of it. Without exception golf pros are Chauvinist Pigs. "Bring along your five iron" they'll say, adding as you grope for the yellow tee pegs that usually bring you luck, "And you won't need those". (Doesn't the supreme puffed-up git know that you can't hit anything unless it's perched high on a tee peg!)

My first lesson was at the birthplace of The Game, with an old Scotsman, tough as the gorse lining his native fairways, who planted himself astride a kitchen chair opposite me and slashed away with a niblick at my left elbow, shin and ankles for the £5 half hour. My injuries kept me off the course for three months, which I spent in bed on a hot line to my lawyer. Even Nicklaus says his first instructor taught him by holding on to his hair so that he couldn't move his head - and that was a man teaching another man!

No, if you are thinking of sexy hands, strong arms and a suggestive lingering smile, you're taking up the wrong game. And if you find the right one, **please** let me know what it is.

Golf for The Girls

On the whole I'd say that, if you haven't yet been bitten by the golf bug, **don't start**. Like smoking, once you have got the habit it is the devil to break. And your whole life will be changed after once having taken that first tentative step on to the practice ground.

One woman I know had surgery (much against her husband's tearful entreaties) to remove 6" off each boob because it was affecting the smooth flow of her follow-through. She ended up literally living on the course from the first inch of dull light until she was putting the 18th green with a torch in her mouth. She put their joint account deeply into the red to buy an electric buggy, thus enabling her to get in more rounds per day.

Extreme you think?

Not at all. Once the bug has got you you will find out for yourself. That will be you in the supermarket, bending forwards and working your shoulders from side to side while you're waiting at the checkout. That will be you practising your follow-through while queuing for the teller at the bank. That will be you practising putting into a glass while he is pouring the wine at a candlelit dinner for two at his pad. I entreat you - be forewarned (But meanwhile when you ARE practising putting into a glass, make sure that it is the right kind of glass: don't accept anything less than the finest paper-thin crystal - none of his chain store stuff with a rim like a casserole lid. His carpet is important too: tell him a fine Persian runner is the best).

Encounters with other Lady Members

or, mind how you choose your friends

Never underestimate the importance of making the Right Friends. Most of us were told at our mothers' knees that we would be judged by the companions we kept, and this is never truer than in a Golf Club.

On joining a Club make straight for what is unfailingly displayed on the wall - a long varnished wooden board with the name of the Lady Captains inscribed thereon, against the year in which they held this exalted office. This board can usually be found in the mixed bar or, if a larger Club, on the walls of the main lounge. Without too obviously seeming to do so, make a thorough mental note of the names of all past Lady Captains whom you think might reasonably be expected to be still alive. If you happen to have an immense memory, add to your list those names appearing as winners of any trophies important enough in the life of the Club to warrant similar boards, which you will find displayed nearby. If, for instance, you notice amongst the Trophy Winners that a Mrs. F.A. (no T?) Bottome has won the St. Valentine Trophy for the last four years, you must rate her high on your "cultivation" list.

Naturally, having identified Mrs. Bottome or last year's Lady Captain, you dare not approach them for a game. One's flesh creeps at the thought. But buy them tea, ask if they have any grandchildren or invite them to a Tupperwear party. This is a sort of insurance policy - if you never get to be a half-decent golfer, you can settle for being considered a sympathetic kindly person who makes delicious scones,

and might even be asked to help check golf scores on Medal Day, Briefly, you are **IN**.

Without helpful and considered advice like this you could find yourself, on your first terrifying day, slap up against the Oldest Member who, I do hasten to add, will not be the loveable old gent who watches the romance of it all from his comfortable armchair on the terrace, as P.G. Wodehouse would have us believe, but a gimlet-eyed thin-lipped weatherbeaten female with brown sinewy arms with a handshake on the end like a steel clamp. She may, out of boredom or sheer energy (having only played 36 holes that morning and glimpsing the departure homewards for lunch of the only other Member in sight) suggest a game.

Suggest a game! What am I saying? *Demand*, rather, that you proceed at once with her to the first tee, and thereafter through a terrifying ordeal that will stay in your mind (and occasionally cause you to wake screaming) until your Last Great Hole is played.

It is useless to protest to such a person that you have eighteen people coming to dinner and all the shopping to do. Useless to protest that you have just had 40 stitches removed from your left leg. Useless to say that you've just moved house and the furniture is arriving in half an hour and that you'd only stopped off at the Club to have a pee. She will press on tee-wards with tank-like singlemindedness, shoulders hunched and with sparks flying from the wheels of her trolley.

Hang on to your Membership.

M ost Clubs have a waiting list of several years, the main reason for which is to discourage too many middle aged housewives whose children are now safely off their hands from cluttering up the fairways and swiping away at balls, being a danger to themselves and everybody else - including innocent passing motorists. So, you will see, you have to decide to be a Lady Golfer about ten or twelve years before you actually become one.

Golf for The Girls

And, whereas it is extremely difficult to become a Member of a Club, it is childishly simple to get thrown out of one. So, once IN you must constantly be on your guard. In the Clubhouse, for instance, it is advisable to stick to coffee in case, after a second sherry, your tongue might loosen and deep hidden resentments about, say, a Member of the Committee, or the lack of toilet paper in the Ladies, might come tumbling wantonly out. One never knows *who* are the Moles, or whether the bar counter is bugged. Quite excepting myself, I have known many ladies who were, shall we say, "dismissed".

One, I recall, was thrown out for exposing herself to a caddy (she had merely found it urgent and necessary to "crouch" behind a fixed hazard). In her case, however, the Caddies Union hastened to have her reinstated, but that particular case has never ceased to amaze me because the caddies I seem to get are so utterly disinterested that I could leap stark naked from a bunker without them even noticing. Their interest in one is usually reduced to asking, with a sigh, when one is trying to concentrate on one's 15th shot down the first fairway, whether one is intending to play the whole 18 holes.

Caddies of course, with few notable exceptions, are always male. Why not female caddies, who understand about our tight knicker elastic, etc? Lady caddies eager to leap into the rough like excited terriers to find one's ball; who'll take over the dreary business of marking the score card with one's interests at heart; who'll discretely re-arrange the lie of one's ball with a delicate and balletic toe.

But, to return briefly to the thin thread by which your continued Club Membership hangs at all times, I'll recount the sad story of a lady member at one of my previous Clubs.

She was a Dutch lady and, being Dutch, pronounced all her "s's" as "sh's" - thus, for instance, she would say "shocks come in sheveral shizes" instead of "socks come in several sizes", should she have wanted for any reason to make such an observation.

Well, my Dutch friend and I had booked a starting time in the approved fashion and she was about to drive off on the first when the irate Lady Captain loomed upon us, purple of visage, steel-grey hair springing from her hairnet.

"We're due to go off before you," she boomed, elbowing her way on to the tee.

"That ish not right," pointed out my friend, reasonably. "We are down on the time sheet for 10 o'clock sharp, which ish now."

"If you had looked at the sheet properly," shouted the Lady Captain, pulling out my friend's peg and chucking it into a herbaceous border, "you would have seen that we were due to go off before you."

"And", said my courageous friend, "if **you** had been **here** on time, instead of **shitting** about in the Change Room..."

We never played that game. She was thrown out for using abusive language to the Lady Captain.

Partners (Choosing)

Women come in lots of different types, far more than of pebbles on the beach, so you will have to use all your analytical and psychological skills in choosing a suitable and sympathetic partner to accompany you around the course dependant, of course, on your standard of play. If you are just about to start off on your first 18 holes, the tendency is to be grateful to anyone who volunteers to spend the next eight or nine hours by your side, but this grabbing hold of the first offer is a great mistake and can ruin your whole attitude to golf for the rest of your life.

A seemingly charming lady might well start off overflowing with caring concern and a desire to give a helping hand to a new member who is struggling to put in cards and get her name up as a 36+. But after she has waited whilst you take 20 shots to hack out of the rough a few yards from the first tee, she may turn into something very different indeed: an ogress reminiscent of those in Brothers Grimm.

This, you will have to admit, will not help you to concentrate or to remember all those things you have been learning about keeping calm and relaxed whilst getting out of the rough. It is more likely that, after two or three holes, you will be overcome with the desire to beat her about the ears with your five iron before striding over her comatose form and smashing your whole set of clubs one by one against the nearest tree.

Lower handicap players will sympathise with your partner as what indeed can be more trying, on a cold and windy day, than to stand around for hours on frozen feet waiting for a beginner to attempt to get her ball into something remotely resembling "play". All right. So why do these women even volunteer, why don't they just laugh in your face when you are touting around for a partner? The reason is simple: every woman likes to project herself in the first instance as caring and considerate even if, in the long run, she hasn't a prayer of being able to keep it up.

If you can't afford to go round with a pro, or can't find a pro willing to take you around no matter how much you offer to pay him, then your best bet is to stick to another learner and, with instruction books in hand, bumble around with her - ducking out of the way and calling through all the proper players coming along behind you.

It's no use looking to husbands/lovers/brothers for help. The most you'll get from them is "just watch the way I do it" when you come across them on the practice ground. You may have spent the best years of your life washing and ironing their clothes, cooking their meals, doing their dishes, cleaning their houses and planting out their gardens but, when it comes to patient assistance on the golf course - you can forget it.

The choice of the right partner is critically important throughout your golf career, even when the day finally comes when your handicap is down and you feel more or less confident that you can give anyone, within reason, a decent game. It should always be a game that you enjoy playing and well worth all the lugging around of trolleys and clubs and bags and boots and changes of clothing several times a week that it incurs, so the companions you choose to share these times with are vitally important.

Its a serious business, so you don't want a partner who will bore you deaf with tales of her holiday in the south of France and pull out great sheaves of snaps on the 13th tee when you're trying to decide which club to take. Neither do you want complete and utter silence for the entire round, which closes your mind to all thoughts other than whether perhaps she took offence at that **** word you

Golf for The Girls

used when you went into the bunker at the 1st. Nerves, you will find, are always close to the surface on the golf course and casual remarks you could get away with around the fireside can make life long enemies of golf partners.

It is not too extreme to say that the person you chose to play golf with should be someone you could happily spend your life with, so attuned must you be to each other's personalities.

People to particularly avoid are (1) doting grandmothers (2) cookery fanatics and (3) twitchers although, with the last category you can take into consideration the "plus" factor of opportunities to improve the lie of your ball whilst she is gazing up a tree or shading her eyes to follow the distant flight of some uncommon species. As to the other two categories, you will agree that talk of the cutting of some damp and bald baby's new tooth or whether or not to add the wretched dill or the blooming cayenne before or after boiling isn't going to help you to focus on the matter on hand, which is getting your ball into that hole with the minimum number of swings.

Ocean-going sailors are excellent company, though they are totally immune to weather and inclined to keep on playing in complete disregard of torrential rain and a force 10 gale when your unequally trained body longs to beat a hasty retreat to the clubhouse, dry socks and a few stiff drinks.

Female executives tend to be bossy, journalists in a desperate hurry to meet deadlines have you running flat out along the fairways, mothers ditto to collect children from school, physiotherapists off-putting with talk of back strain, doctors are likely to be on call and interrupt your game just when you're getting into it and shop keepers, of course, ingrained to tell you that you are always right - which is palpable nonsense.

So what do you look for? That's a good question - and I hope you find the answer.

Sinister Activities in the Locker Room

It is all too easy to be hoodwinked into a state of false security by the offer of an orange flavoured glucose sweet from a gently smiling lady competitor. But one must be constantly on one's guard.

Before the Monthly Medal, burrs have been found stuffed down the toes of golf shoes, hairnets have been sprayed with glue, knicker elastic tightened, wasps pushed into golf gloves and, you may remember the famous occasion of the Lady Captain's Trophy when sneezing powder was sprinkled into the Lady Secretary's golf bag. Even more recently, and at the same Club, ground glass was discovered, alas too late, in the barley water at a Happy Families Mixed Foursome.

So, greatest vigil should be exercised at all times, particularly as the culprits, if apprehended and challenged, will merely accuse you of being a spoil sport. It is only, they will giggle and nudge each other, girlish high spirits.

If you are normally in the habit of leaving clothes and equipment at your Club I suggest that, before a Medal meeting, you remove everything to your home for a thorough inspection and, on the day, prepare for the match in your car with the doors locked on the inside. This isn't especially comfortable in hot weather and one's shoe laces tend to tangle around the gear lever and one's golf balls to rush into those inaccessible places under the seats. But, on the whole, I consider it sound practice.

Just to underline how very serious I am about all this, I don't recommend letting it be commonly known around the Clubhouse that you have made provision in your Will for a wooden bench with a brass plaque to be installed at the 11th tee.

Golf for The Girls

This business of preparing yourself for a match is of an importance impossible to underestimate. Above I have dealt with guarding your golfing clothes and equipment, but the fact must be faced that when you step on to the first tee, whether or not your name will go out in the Newsletter as the Medal Winner is entirely up to you - so, to prepare yourself emotionally, physically and psychologically for the Match is of vital importance.

Remember that the "Hi girls - gosh, I'm late!" attitude never won anybody a gold wrapped Dunlop 65.

A week before the match I recommend soaking the hands and feet in warm scented water three or four times a day. The water must not be too hot as this tends to weaken the muscles - the elbow test remains the best, as for babies.

Clear the mind absolutely of all problems which, I find, can only be done by saying a firm "Shh" to anyone who tries to start a conversation. Don't read newspapers, especially the financial section and horoscopes. Eat out at good restaurants being sure to pass the bill to someone else. Go to bed early with a light romantic novel (Barbara Cartland will do). If you can afford to buy yourself new golf clothes this will help your morale, but do remember what I have said about these: good sexless hand-knitted jerseys can be found in charity shops.

On the day of the Match, after a light breakfast in bed, take a long warm bath and lie full length on the floor with your arms above your head and listen to classical music (not Wagner - and don't start on a full Symphony unless you have drawn a late starting time). The arms above the head is important because this will confirm that you can get them there.

Having already cleaned your golf shoes and pinged out the pebbles from under your shoes with the pointed end of a nail file, you should be ready.

Arrive at the Club in good time, but not early enough to be tempted on to the putting green, or undo all the good you have done whilst listening to Mozart, by hurling drives into the practice net. Walk gracefully to the first tee and shake everybody's hand cooly and firmly. (As you shake with the right hand this will not have a detrimental affect on your grip. If you're

Focus - it might not help, but it is terribly trendy.

left handed, ignore that bit). The surprise of having their hands shaken cooly but firmly, like this, which is not normal Golf Club practice before a game, will do a great deal towards confusing and flustering your opponents. They, you will find, will raise their eyebrows nervously at each other while you alone remain calm and in full control. Practice maintaining an enigmatic smile.

The great moment has come - and you are prepared.

On studying these points of hitherto ungiven advice to lady golfers you may wonder why it hasn't started off by dealing with such matters as the grip, swing, stance, bunker shots, chip shots, etc. etc. as you will no doubt have found explained in great detail to men in their golf books. Much of this may be dealt with later, but it is of primary importance at the outset to know and understand Golf Club Life, thus avoiding the many pitfalls and, at the same time, winning early advantages.

Golf for The Girls

Consider, for instance, that advice of this nature is never given to men, who blunder in and out of their Clubs like junior school boys at tea break, completely oblivious of the dark subterranean machinations of much older and subtler members.

How often one sees the poor things, after a game, sitting in their cars staring sightlessly into space wondering whatever happened - where they have gone wrong. Whilst others, lacking that extra degree of energy necessary to propel them to their cars, slump with sad bewildered expressions in clubhouse armchairs, cradling double gins, or wildly playing the fruit machines in a teeth-clenched frenzy to re-establish their superiority over the world which, as we all know, is a condition necessary to men.

It is unsuitable for a lady to behave in such a manner so, before she even starts on the long long uphill grind towards becoming a competent performer on the course, the aspiring lady golfer must have faced up to and learned how to avoid the snares littering the path on the way to her chosen goal.

The wisdom of this will now seem obvious, so let us proceed.

6

Slow Play

or, Don't Stop to Tie Up your Shoelace

The creeping horror of Slow Play is never far from the thoughts of any Club golfer. When practised it has the power to drive even the mildest of golfers into an uncontrollable frenzy. Meetings are held about it in Golf Clubs the length and breadth of the land; Professionals of the highest standing are penalised for it; backs are turned on, or icy glances directed towards Offenders when they plod exhausted into the clubhouse; extremely rude remarks are made in stage whispers in the bar, and anonymous letters are slipped at dead of night under the door of the Secretary's office.

So never be caught committing this - the most deadly - **Sin**. Face up to the fact that if you send your ball flying into the rough, no matter what the Rules say, you are positively not going to be allowed any time to look for it by the four ball sprinting down the fairway behind you, belting their balls at the speed of death past your ears. Your only defence is to crouch down in the long grass with your hands protectively over your head and let them come storming past.

Once you have thus given up your place in the mad stampede it might mean that you won't have a chance to resume your peaceful game for five or six hours. The advantage, however, is that you may, from your crouched position in the rough, not only find your own ball, but several quite good ones that have been hastily abandoned by players ahead of you. So use up this time by scrambling around on all fours and, if you have an old pair of tights in your golf bag, you will find them most useful for storage.

Why Slow Play should be regarded as the Ultimate Sin for golfers has never been satisfactorily explained to me. Golf is a game which was invented to be played leisurely with friends, a game lasting half a day, followed by drinks and a good meal. A pleasant social occasion which got everyone out in the fresh air.

So what happened to golf? With the exception of squash, which everyone accepts one just rushes out and plays at great speed followed by a noisy shower and the next party, most games follow a leisurely pattern. Although a maximum of four people only can play a game of tennis, whoever heard of the next match slamming on to the court in the middle of a game, shoving the first players aside? Cricketers always have long breaks for eating cucumber sandwiches and drinking tea, and whoever minds how long they take changing their jerseys and chatting on the cricket field? Even footballers frequently stop play to cuddle and kiss each other; rugby players gather in endless scrums to exchange the latest jokes until someone remembers to kick the ball out backwards. But golf, these days, has to be played at high speed, thus the use of the small motorcars (buggies) we find on all American courses, a practice that is fast spreading across the Atlantic and one which will eventually price the game beyond the limits of our housekeeping money.

But to consider the other side of the coin, I won't say that it isn't extremely annoying if you are immediately behind a very slow match and you have a deadline to get home and put on the roast. So it pays to keep an eye on the group ahead and, if you see them surreptitiously uncorking a bottle of wine amongst those pine trees on the 8th, adopt avoiding tactics: i.e. move to other tees, playing any hole that is available. This, of course, can lead to total confusion over the whole course, but at least you will get the joint in the oven on time.

For reasons above-stated, jogging is an exercise to be recommended for golfers. Once you get into the rhythm of jogging you will find you can do it easily around the course, pausing only for addressing and swinging. Club selection, if you are seriously going in for it, can be achieved while jogging on the spot, rather like prize fighters do.

For those of us who prefer a relaxed and thoughtful game, I suggest two holes at dawn and another two at dusk. This will mean (I think, but you can check me out) that it will take you four and a half days to complete 18 holes, but will give you the opportunity to apply the necessary amount of care and concentration whilst playing.

Rhythm

some got it.

Rhythm is very important and is, like "style", something you either have or haven't got. If you have rhythm, and remember that you have it when you are out there, you'll have a great advantage over the girls and boys who haven't got it. And if your general music appreciation is of the pre-Beatles era, you'll be even better off. Try and keep your musical thoughts on Strauss and Lehar. Standing on the first tee with the outpourings of the latest pop star going through your head isn't nearly so beneficial as the music you still remember fondly from your Olde Tyme dancing class. So fix your mind firmly on The Blue Danube.

Try this with me now. Imagine you are teed up and about to start your backswing...

"Where the blue
(*whilst you are doing your backswing*)
DAN...
(*the "Dan" is when you swing through the ball*)
...UBE"
(*that's for the beautiful high follow through*)

...see, there it goes - sailing straight down the middle.

And take it SLOWLY. If it helps you can sing it aloud, grunting the "Dan" rather like present-day tennis players.

But while you are singing, don't forget to keep your head down, your left arm straight, your elbows in, your grip tight but not too tight, your left foot horizontal to the fairway and slightly back, the back of your left hand facing the flag and the V between the thumb and forefinger of your right hand pointing over your right shoulder.

Good luck!

8

Rules

They have ways of making people obey them

One of the worst things one can do to an enthusiastic budding lady golfer is to make her a present of the Rule Book unless, of course, for one reason or another you want her to give up. For instance for a husband whose wife is threatening to take up the game, and thereby generally queer his pitch at the Golf Club, to assess the danger in good time and present his wife with a copy of the Rule Book would be a stroke of pure genius.

At first, when she throws her arms around his neck and thanks him lovingly for his present, he might think he has made a terrible mistake. However, the 120 odd pages of fairly small print sets out all the things you are not allowed to do on the course, plus the punishments, ranging from merely losing a stroke, to losing two strokes or even the hole, through to downright disqualification. And when she realises the penalities apply not only for the player but also "the side", she will go back into the kitchen, trembling to think of what a narrow escape she has had.

Imagine the disgrace! - the shame, dishonour, scandal of having to return head-bowed to the Clubhouse with that terrible word "disqualified" ringing in one's ears. Imagine the other member of one's "side", glaring through tear stained eyes and the subsequent talk over the tea-cups. No gently nurtured, sensitive woman could face it.

But then, of course, there are the other kind of women, not so gently nurtured or sensitive whose eyes glint like points of steel at the thought of a challenge and who, if disqualified for some infringement of the Rules, would throw back her head and, grabbing her "side" by the arm, happily make for the bar and the extra gin-and-tonic time happily to be spent while the rest of the gang thunder around the course.

But before even looking at the Rules, there is Course Etiquette to be learned and the first thing we are told is not to swing a club when there is someone standing near enough to be hit by it. An easy enough thing to avoid doing on the first tee, but a courtesy which might become more and more tempting to forego later on in the game.

Other rules of etiquette are fairly basic and for the sake of peace we can go along with them, but the one about not leaning on one's putter in order to get the ball out of the hole poses a problem. Lots of ladies couldn't get the ball out of the hole unless some outside agent was used. How many of us can just bend down with ease to pick up something from the carpet? How many of us can even begin to look at those books on the bottom shelves of the library, without having to haul ourselves ignominiously upright again with the wild use of elbows and knees, clutching at higher shelves as we go. So, to avoid infringement of this courtesy rule, we need to come to an agreement with fellow players: I'll pull you up, and you can pull me up.

Some Rules are so mysterious that only the male mind, who invented them, can interpret them. For instance "The margin of a bunker extends vertically downwards, but not upwards." What on earth to they mean? "Downward" I sort of understand, but I've stood at bunkers looking upwards and can't see any margins. This also applies to water hazards which, we are told, extend vertically upwards and downwards as well. "Downwards" is easier here, you can see the fish, but "upwards"?

And what do they mean by "manufactured ice"? Do players really go around emptying their ice trays all over the course? Obviously they do, or it wouldn't be mentioned in the Rules as an obstruction.

And this business about getting off the green as soon as possible, having first quickly replaced the flag and rushed around tidying up pitch marks and spike marks to leave it all nice and tidy for the next chaps. All right, but we are then told that, when we think it is all over at the l8th green, the dreaded disqualification is threatened if we leave the putting green having not first sorted out some dispute about failing to hole out. You can imagine what ages this might take and the accompanying pantomime conversation "Oooh yes she did" and "Oooh no she didn't" while the match behind quietly curl up on the grass and go to sleep.

The Rule Book needs to be taken in small, controlled doses. Just read two or three and sleep on them, returning refreshed the next morning to tackle a couple more. If you pick it up and read it from cover to cover I absolutely guarantee that you'll never go near a golf course again - your addiction will be cured. Although not actually written in legal language, it is couched in such a way that the average woman reader, more used to reading horoscopes and those delicious scandals in the popular press, will literally feel her brain gradually tangle up until it is in a tight little ball somewhere behind her left ear.

Repair Your Pitch Marks.

This rule hardly ever concerns lady golfers. Personally I've never landed on a green from such a height and with such force as to make a pitch mark, which is extremely sad because I have carried that little fork-ended tool around in my pants' pocket, often quite painfully, for nigh on twenty years without the sublime and heady pleasure of stepping onto the green needing to use it.

Approach shots, I find, generally either trickle to a halt on the front fringe of the green, or race wildly across and into the far bunker, scattering one's opponents balls (which have been waiting there for some time) like the beginning of a snooker frame.

Please Replace Divots.

A s one sweet old lady once said to me, "If I knew what divots were, my dear, I'd gladly replace them."

A divot, I'll explain for the benefit of absolute beginners, is the small piece of turf gouged out of the ground on those rare occasions when you have neither a fresh air shot nor do you top the ball. This piece of turf may then fly through the air landing, worms upward, a few yards away and I agree (with reservations) that these pieces of turf should be replaced in the ground from whence they came and trodden down with some force.

Golf for The Girls

Reservations? My reservation is that a certain type of lady, the superefficient housewife type, should be excused from obeying this rule. We have all seen them, crawling around the fairways on three fours with one arm full of divots as they look for holes in the fairway which exactly fit each one. I have even observed one of these neurotic housewives, on finding herself with a divot left over, gouging a perfect hole in the virgin turf to accommodate it.

It is easy to see what chaos would result if a Club were to have twenty or so such housewives turning up on Ladies Day: something more resembling a vast open air knitting party or a giant jig-saw than a game of golf, whilst the sweep-it-under-the-carpet type of housewives lounge around in bunkers smoking cigarettes watching their more exacting sisters seek amongst each others' collections for exactly the right divot.

So this rule, though fundamentally a sound one, should be tempered with reason.

Putting

It's nothing like it used to be at the seaside

There are a whole lot of gestures and rules applying to greens. One is not supposed to walk with spiked shoes between where an opponents ball lies, and the cup. If, of course, your opponent turns around to blow her nose or check where the two-ball behind you has got to, it is all right to jump up and down on her line of putt until it resembles a straightened out kitchen colander.

But this is not advisable if playing with an opponent who wears highly polished spectacles through which she might catch a reflection of your behaviour, or when playing with a very evil tempered man.

Prolong your putting for as long as you can. Walk slowly all around the green, studying your shot from every angle. Crouch down with your putter blade like a pendulum in front of you even if, like me, you have not the faintest idea what this is supposed to prove.

Fling yourself full length face down on the grass with your nose close to your ball and carefully study each blade of grass between you and the cup. Once again, I have no idea what burst of knowledge this is supposed to relay to your brain, but can assure you that it does tend to undermine your opponent and is, therefore, well worth the discomfort of lying for several minutes on your stomach with squashed boobs. Then - and only then - line up for your putt, being sure that before placing your putter behind the ball you place it in front of your ball, as this confuses people and makes them think you are going to putt in the wrong direction. The reason behind all these activities on the green need not be understood except as excellent delaying and undermining tactics, which has to be good enough reason for anybody.

Only when you have done all these things, with leisure and style, and can see your opponent biting her bottom lip, her face getting redder and her hands starting to tremble ever so slightly, do you actually put blade to ball.

Much can be learned from watching the line your opponent's ball takes, and this can best be done by standing behind her. Even better results can be gained by taking a step forward as she moves her putter blade into the back position.

The greens are where the Dunlop 65's are lost and won. So, in addition to the procedures mentioned above, a few additional suggestions are given below:

- a few quiet sneezes (quiet ones being more irritating than full-blooded ones)
- make sure your shadow crosses your opponents line of putt; remember that a moving shadow is worth more points to you than a stationary one.
- always stand where she can see any movement you make out of the corner of her eye.
- if you are tending the flag, jiggle it about.
- wave to somebody on the next tee

That will start you off and give you the general idea, you can think of additional variations on this theme for yourselves.

10

Coarse Architecture.

Standing on any tee at any Golf Course, looking down the fairway towards the green, you will realise (if you haven't long ago realised) that all Course Architects are men.

Let us consider first of all the bunkers (or traps, depending on your religion) on a par-four hole. The nearest one, with an overhanging lip like Mick Jagger's, you will find well to the fore of the average male golfer's range of drive but placed exactly where the average lady golfer's drive is likely to land. So you must face up to the fact that the first ten minutes or so of your game will certainly be spent thrashing about trying to dig yourself out and to a position somewhere on the fairway.

When this is achieved, and you've shaken and brushed yourself more or less free of sand, and used your eyedropper, you take another look and find the next gaping bunker, a sneaky little stream or a large oak tree in the exact spot where your second shot has a fair chance of terminating.

This second trap/stream/tree is, of course, merely an object of charm and beauty to your male opponent whose drive left him positioned just comfortably close and easily able to land his second shot if not by the flag then a safe little chip away from it.

So, after your second shot, you are either smashing about in sand again, ankle keep in muddy water or trying to figure out how to get from under a tree with no room for any kind of backswing. Your male partner, meanwhile, isn't helping by standing on the green sighing, with his hands on his hips.

The next hole is a par-three. Glancing at it you realise, with tears springing to your eyes, that in no possible way is your drive going to land on the green. Even using every known muscle and bicep along with some you haven't even discovered yet you are destined to land, without any doubt whatsoever, in that sneering fringe of bunkers (traps) or in that dark fathomless lake that the architect has put there just for you.

So you sniff, brush away the tears, wiggle your driver (the men are using nine irons) and extend your shoulders to such a degree that you won't be able to do any ironing for six weeks and - whoosh!

Well, I was right, wasn't I?

The par-five's are just a joke, as you will realise as you stand on the tee and observe (should you happen to be extremely far-sighted) a tiny coloured speck far away in the distant hills which your wryly smiling male opponent will hasten to tell you is the flag. If, you muse to yourself, you take your customary minimum of three putts, this means you have to be alongside that distant dot after your drive and one fairway wood. Supposing always of course that your drive should happen to leave you in a position to play a fairway wood, which, you safely assume, it won't, for the simple reason that any halfwit can see that between where you are standing and that distant coloured dot are bunkers & water hazard. Not to mention narrow strips of fairway with horrendous rough snuggling all along it, trees, quarries, and clumps of nasty looking rock carefully arranged by the architect to catch the limited range of the lady golfer.

If you have far sight, you will just have been watching your male opponent's ball (on this hole his tee is only slightly behind yours) which is now sitting smugly on a special plateau arranged by the architect for this purpose, safe from all hazards and dangers and with only a long-iron shot needed to put it on the green.

This diabolical placing of hazards continues through the eighteen holes so, we can't fail but ask ourselves, why not lady Course Architects who, with sly little giggles, will arrange those hazards just that bit further away,or nearer, to catch our smirking self-important male opponents?

Ah but, say the men, we give you ladies the tremendous advantage of having your tees placed well ahead of ours, thus shortening the holes for you. This, friends, is rubbish and, on the rare occasions when their tees are a decent bit behind ours, it is merely done to give us an inferiority complex before we even start on our rendering of the Blue Danube (see chap.8).

It is all part of the psychological warfare of the mixed game. As we walk towards the first tee, having watched the menfolk slam their balls far into the distance, we find ourselves feeling less and less important in the great scheme of things. On arriving, we can only wonder what on earth we are doing there and how much happier we would be, freed of all competition and with our feet up and our noses in a good book.

And this is quite the wrong state of mind because we all know that the most important thing is to have confidence for a good drive at the first tee, even if we know in our hearts that the whole thing will degenerate into a sick joke afterwards.

A certain type of male is passionately in tune with nature and aware of beauty, given to dancing alone in moonlit gardens with a single rose between his teeth. (Don't you believe me? Its true!). Alas, such members of their sex rarely if ever take up golf, so we can be fairly sure that the ones we draw to play with in our competitions will be of the more earthy variety. It is therefore extremely important that you kerb your love of nature whilst you are out there. If there is an adorable little rabbit with a white fluffy tail sitting between you and the pin - aim for it. Stray dogs and cantering horses are also fair game. Completely banish all your natural female sensitivity. You won't be thanked for shrieking "Oh look!

Golf for The Girls

Quick! There's a ring-necked purple feathered swallow tit!" when your male partner is working on a nasty little tricky chip to the green.

And if a nightingale should sing - ignore it and keep your head down. Remember the woman who was barred from the second round of the Jolly Foursomes Week Trophy for deliberately moving her ball on the fairway. "It was," she quietly explained to a table full of bulging eyed committee members, "squashing such a pretty little mauve flower".

As our golf balls rarely land where we are aiming them we need not be afraid that our fairways will be littered with decapitated squirrels and confused motherless fledglings. A perfect example of a true lady golfer's dedication and disregard of nature was seen on a course in South America. She was about to make a difficult chip from the edge of a water hazard when her opponent, ashen faced, quietly pointed out that the log in front of her was an alligator. Such concern was rewarded by a steely glance and the shot was played with care and precision, after

"I've met worse in the changing rooms"

which the lady stepped over the alligator and, without a backward glance, proceeded in pursuit of her ball on its unerring course towards the flag.

Nobody, except fishermen, really like worms, so these can be readily crushed under ones spikes. Only the more squeamish walk around them.

And so: leaves turning red in the autumn sunlight, vistas of rolling hills, willows sleepily nodding over deep still pools, rainbows, grazing deer, the wonderful precision flight of migrating birds - all these things, like the nightingale, must be ignored.

Total concentration comes much easier to men than to women because, as we all know, they have less on their minds. Once they have walked out of their offices, blowing a farewell kiss to their secretaries, their minds are like large unpatterned king sized sheets after a whiter than white washday. We, on the other hand, have our minds cluttered all day and night with problems: collecting the kids from school, have they got clean shirts? pants? socks? how to thicken gravy, how to alter last year's dresses to this year's style, shouldn't one really be at home cleaning the double glazing? what to buy Aunt Mary for her birthday? Well, you know, the list is endless and when one problem is safely solved six others crowd in to take its place.

Complete concentration is, however, absolutely essential on the golf course. If, therefore, you are determined to become the Greatest Lady Golfer, and spend your spare moments away from the course planning what you will say in your acceptance speech when you win your first Major, you must be able to put everything else out of your mind and concentrate utterly and to the exclusion of all else on every single shot that you take.

Second only to concentration is confidence.

Golf for The Girls

Confidence

How to avoid those knocking knees.

Realise when you set off that it is a to-the-death contest between you and the course, and don't let yourself think even for a moment that the course is sure to win.

You must breast your way to that first tee convinced that this time, this day, will be IT: bells will ring in the trees, heavenly choirs will be heard from the rough and the deep swelling chords of a mighty organ will echo from the bunkers. This is going to be The Day. Nothing that might detract you from this Great and Wonderful Ideal should be countenanced.

You sink a 6" putt on the first green. Well, it is no more than you expected, is it? No need to leap in the air shouting "It's in! It's in!" The very least this can do is bring down upon you an elderly red faced Admiral (retired) from where he was about to drive on the second tee, with clenched teeth and extended shaking hands forming the shape of a neck which, you will agree, does nothing for your personal single-minded concentration on this to-the-death battle against the course.

Even our idle thoughts: what we will wear tomorrow night, should we try the new hairdresser, sex, should we enrol in flower arranging classes or musical appreciation, men, should we re-paper the dining room, etc. - all these thoughts must be left with our spongebag in the locker room.

Of course most of us don't aspire to having the likes of Sally Little fall at our feet in wonder and amazement. There are other and lowlier aspirations, like reducing our handicap to 30 or, as is the aim of many more advanced lady golfers, to be appointed Lady Captain.

The main reason behind this desire to be Lady Captain is obvious: as Lady Captain one can park one's car slap up against the clubhouse in a reserved parking bay, instead of having to join in the general confusion of the car park - usually ending up as far away from the ladies' change room as it is possible to get - and having to make one's way half a mile in often foul and muddy weather.

Another great advantage as Lady Captain is that you have your name up on the board I mentioned or, better still, in some Clubs a carefully posed coloured and framed picture (with the wrinkles smoothed out by a kindly and sympathetic photographer).

An additional advantage, of course, is that you get lots of members anxious to buy you a gin and tonic and a sausage roll, which means that more housekeeping money might be spent on things like golf balls and assimilated leather score card holders.

I would warn you, however, that there are certain tedious tasks involved in this office so, unless you have an intelligent son or daughter anxious to take these on in return for your turning a blind eye to what time they come in at night, I'd be inclined to give the whole thing a miss. For instance, you have to know about scoring.

Scoring is an extremely difficult aspect of golf for the average lady golfer. So, if you feel you can trust the men in your four ball, it is advisable to let them handle it, thus avoiding ferocious scenes in the clubhouse afterwards with, in the background, your tiny polite voice murmuring "oh but John dear, I've distinctly got on the card that you had a nine at the fourth, not a four." This sort of thing does not add to harmony in the home.

Golf for The Girls

Scoring, as I say, is very difficult and complicated, so much so that I hesitate to mention it as it can only add to your confusion - and mine.

Match play I did begin to understand once. Or was it match play? Anyway, it went something like you work out the difference between the handicaps of the players adding two together and taking away the other two and then the difference between them indicates which holes the first two have a stroke or two strokes on as indicated on the card. Do you understand? Oh well.

As regards one's own score, if just playing a friendly game with a dear old mate many women take along that little gadget used on the end of knitting needles for counting stitches, but I have found that men tend to look askance at this, so it is advisable to turn one's back whilst doing it. But after shyly turning your back in bunkers and under trees and things you'll find, men being what they are, that they tend to sidle up to you to see what you are doing hoping, one has to think, you are having trouble with your fly zip or your shirt has come undone at the most interesting button.

A kindly uncle once gave me a special golf stroke counter fashioned in the shape of a round dial with a metal pointer - rather like a clock with one hand. The disadvantage of this was it only counted up to a hundred and I found that I had used up most of it on the first five holes. By the time I had completed the course I had forgotten how many times I had been round the dial.

It is considered irritating, especially when playing with men, to ask around the green how many shots they think you have had. The best system is to keep saying to yourself "this is my seventh" or "this is my eighth" as you toil along, handing in with a sigh what you think is an honest total to the chap with the pencil waiting on the green. If you listen quietly to the men you will hear that the correct scoring of a golf contest sounds like the stock exchange on a busy Monday, so try and keep as remote as possible from this unpleasant aspect of the royal and ancient game.

Golf for The Girls

Sex on the Golf Course.

Although P.G.Wodehouse would have us believe that young Lord Algenon, heir to the Milksop Millions, is perpetually chasing the dimpled charms of the Hon. Prunella with steaming breath down the fairways and in and out amongst the trees, that is not only fiction but fiction from a more romantic era.

In real life there is no sex on the golf course. Nothing can deter us from admiring those powerful shoulders and taut stomach muscles discernible through tee shirts and snug trousers on the men's tees, or from wistfully looking at the caress of those firm gentle hands as they reverently fold them around the grip, but it is advisable to keep such weakening admiration under tight control.

You will find that having sexual vapours on the tee and having to cast about for your smelling salts will not cause any one of those god-like creatures to be overcome with lust and carry you off to a quiet corner of the clubhouse. So forget about it.

I would go so far as to suggest that you don't play golf with your husband/boy friend/lover, or any man you are hoping might one day become any one of these.

Countless steaming love affairs and happy tranquil marriages have been irreparably broken up over little things like failure to sink a 2" putt, taking 15 shots to get out of a bunker or by simply emitting a (loud) sigh during his backswing.

I have seen a really lovely husband stand screaming down, scarlet faced, at his wife, a sobbing speck at the bottom of a disused quarry "Take your wedge you sill old cow and get that ....ing ball back on the fairway!" during a friendly Sunday afternoon mixed foursome. (N.B. In most good Clubs bad language is discouraged, but men are, neverthe-less, allowed to swear at their wives).

If you have ever wondered why in most good Clubs there is an exclusively male bar, this is to give them time to simmer down after the game, thus ensuring that the Ladies Section is not bloodily depleted of too many of its Members after a mixed match. This is on the whole an excellent idea as it also gives the lady members a chance to apologise amongst themselves for the brutish behaviour of their husbands.

So remember to curb all your natural warm female instincts. Don't slip your hand coyly into the crook of your opponent's arm and look lovingly up into his eyes as your fourball walks towards the starting tee, even if he should look amazingly like a bronzed Ballesteros.

If you should see a 6 ft. blond and tanned god striding down the next fairway, don't throw down your golf bag and rush off across the rough in hot pursuit because he'll be concentrating 100% on his game and if he should notice you at all it will only be to demand with ill-concealed anger what the hell you think you're doing charging about and getting into everybody's way.

At all times and in the face of whatever overwhelming temptation keep a controlled distance, no matter how this goes against your natural healthy desires. Should you happen to have one of these bronzed and beautiful gods at your Club, wait for him to depart and take a note of his car number. This way you can keep an eye out and corner him in the village post office, the dog training class or some similar neutral ground.

Another suggestion is an apparently casual enquiry from the stew-ard at the bar, where he will certainly be known. You could, for example, say that he looks just like your long-lost cousin Fred. A really well trained steward will then reply "His name is Alexander Peregrine Fortesque, 6'4", divorced, two children, successful solicitor, lives at the White House on Puffin Common, parents dead, keeps a live-in manservant, plays golf Tues, Thurs and Sats at 2 p.m. and has just ended an unhappy relation-ship with a librarian." You see how easy it could be.

You may be wondering what all that has to do with golf. The answer is it is merely to underline the necessity of keeping everything, even the most fundamental, that has not a direct bearing on your game, quite ruthlessly in its proper place.

Practice Practising

Practising the full golf swing is not easy if you live in a high rise apartment block. Some, of course, have balconies but these are generally so narrow that there is a very real danger that you'll go head first over the railing if your practice swing has anything like the proper extension.

In your sitting room the practice swing can only amount to anything by first removing the coffee table, settee, a few armchairs, casual tables, escritoire and bookcase, even after which there is a reasonable chance of smashing the clubhead through the telly screen.

So, if you have no garden, there are two alternatives: the area allocated for practice at your Club, or a public driving range.

Golf Clubs always have an area put aside for the purpose of practice but not only are these often hazardously placed so that you are in constant danger of being decapitated by one of the balls in play on the adjoining fairway, but one also has the back-breaking business of picking up all one's practice balls afterwards, or those of them that can be found. If you practice at your Club therefore you need a total disregard of danger and several hundred practice balls. The first many of us have naturally, the second is extraordinarily difficult to achieve unless one is prepared to spend all one's spare time hunting around in the rough.

Most Clubs also provide a practice bunker, but whenever I've gone along to try and master the laughingly impossible art of the bunker shot, I've found a noisy group of other women with the same idea in mind, all thrashing about, shouting and waving their deadly sand irons in the air.

The same applies to the practice green, the surface of which, you may have noticed, is never tended lovingly like the greens on the course itself, but left to sprout clumps of dandelion and tiny cabbages, between which the odd cynical mole pushes his way up from time to time to see

Golf for The Girls

how we are all getting on. When querying why the practice green bore little resemblance to the real thing one was told that the putting green fulfils this purpose and that that is always immaculate. So where, one wonders, might one practice those rather fun little shots where the ball is supposed to land gently on the green and roll with deadly accuracy towards the pin - especially as our strength is historically supposed to be in our "short game"? The answer, we must darkly assume, is the reason why these practice greens are merely provided and then left to slip back to nature: our short game is feared by ham fisted men who haven't been brought up to roll fishcakes, make light pastry or pin nappies on to delicate babies.

Golf for The Girls

At a driving range one hires a bucket of rather battle scarred but often interestingly painted balls and, standing in a line resembling the starting gate at horse races we can slosh away in the general direction of painted signs which tell us how far we have gone, e.g. 150 yds., 200 yds., etc. Someone goes and picks up he balls afterwards, putting them back into the buckets.

What puts one off driving ranges is that other partakers of this facility, who are usually male because they have more spare time to devote to such pursuits, generally stand around in little groups laughing at one.

When they are not doing this, they'll be practising alongside you, but so close that their backswings brush the pompoms on your golf cap or, more irritatingly, clonk you on the ear. Taking a step backwards to avoid this you are directly in line for the downswing of the chap behind you, which can have quite disastrous results like splintered bones, skin grafts and twelve months removed from competition.

An additional feature at driving ranges is the customary use of rather strange rubber mats into which you are supposed to press your tees. These mats are usually made of strips of wire and very tough rubberised stuff joined together, with gaps cunningly arranged to accept your tees. When the mats are old, the rubber strips are so loosely joined together that the gaps between greedily gobble up the tees which sink right down so that quite a lot of time can be spent crouched down digging them out with a nail file. If the mats are brand spanking new, one needs a screwdriver and hammer to persuade the tees to go in and a small pair of pliers to get them out again. Usually plastic ones are not re-usable as these end up looking like palm trees in a hurricane.

So, as you see, if visiting a driving range it is advisable to take a hammer, a pair of pliers, a small screwdriver, a nailfile and a crash helmet.

If you should pick up the rubber mat an sling it into the next field in order to get down to the good old grass slumbering underneath, an angry driving range keeper will emerge from his little office where he sits with all the buckets of balls and be very angry indeed.

If you have a small garden which has not been given over to growing veggies you are in the happy position of being able to go out there and practice swing to your heart's content. You can swipe away at the heads of daisies, worms, birds' eggs, anything that happens to be lying about. Ignore the solemn row of village children who collect to watch, and the occasional cries of "Cor! Look at 'er."

You can even erect a practice net.

These are extremely good for the morale as, if you stand close enough, most of your practice balls will actually find contact with the net but will leave you smilingly innocent of how far or in what direction they would have gone had they been for real.

You can also buy practice balls with holes in them but this is rather like trying to stiffen egg whites with a broken whisk.

Quite the best way to practice is in a very large garden put to lawns. Achieving this is extremely expensive so you either have to put your life savings on an outsider to come up in the 3.30 or persuade your husband to move to something standing in a couple of acres. The first suggestion has a better chance of working.

Practice WHAT?

Much against the wishes of the pro at my new Club - who has aged noticeably since I became a Member - I really feel it necessary to outline some hidden pitfalls and suggest adjustments the lady golfer must make in order to establish a regular and unvaried approach to the purely physical business of wielding the club and getting the ball to go in the right direction.

Firstly, clubs are very heavy. Take the driver. When you stand for the first time with this extremely long piece of metal topped with a great lump of wood in your hands, a feeling of sheer impossibility comes over you. So the first thing is to make friends with it. Carry it around with you so you get used to the feel of it, like a handbag or an umbrella or one of the other daily trappings of life.

This will not surprise anyone as they'll merely assume you are on your way to get it repaired providing, of course, you don't overdo it and take it to the theatre and dinner parties. At first you'll crack your ankles with it, break your fingernails getting through doors and possibly do some light injury to a few pedestrians but, eventually, you will get used to having it around and the numbing fear you felt on first encountering it will vanish. Then it is time to study the grip.

The grip is most firmly applied by the left hand even if all your instincts are screaming to hold it with the right. I don't really know why this should be so, but I was made to promise my Club pro that I would not neglect to mention it.

Not only must the grip be firmly applied with the left hand, but with the three least important fingers of the left hand, i.e. the pinkie and those two which grow next to it. This may seem quite ridiculous, but I'll refrain from further comment.

Once you have got those three fingers clinging on for dear life you can wrap the other two around to sort of balance it off. The back of the hand should be facing where you hope the ball will finally arrive. If you see your thumb waving about in the air this is wrong as it should be down the shaft helping things along.

Golf for The Girls

So there you are with your left hand firmly in the correct position. Now you have to change it all by making a space between the index and next-to-it fingers of your left hand in order that the little finger of your right hand can snuggle in between them. If you have been trying this as you read, you should now be standing with your left hand and the little finger of your right all tidily tucked away, but with the rest of the fingers of your right hand weaving about in the manner of snakes about to strike, or a caterpillar looking around for the next leaf to get to. So just wrap these around the grip in the most natural way you can find and, with any sort of luck, the V between your right hand thumb and index finger will be pointing over your right shoulder.

Next, squeeze the whole grip tightly, then release it a little so that most of the pressure remains with those hitherto hardly used last three fingers of your left hand, leaving all the other fingers ready to a good back-up job.

Having established a warm friendly relationship with your driver, and with your hands in the positions indicated, you are now ready to take some practice swings.

As most women are actresses at heart, it is of the utmost importance that you watch and copy golfers with good swings and avoid watching and copying those with bad swings. If you happen to be on the tee with, or are watching from the clubhouse, a bad swinger - cover your eyes.

Video tape some good swingers, watching them for hours and emulating them in front of your full length mirror when there is nobody around. You will find watching yourself in the mirror, whilst at the same time keeping your head down, is extremely difficult and can cause a serious squint in the left eye. Avoiding this may mean that you have to rig up mirrors all around the walls, floor and ceiling, but you will agree that the resulting golf star that will emerge will more than justify the expense.

The absolute grace and poetry of Mr. Faldo is blissful watching material but you must remember that he is a man, with different kinds of muscles, legs, etc. So get hold of a tape of Mrs. Lopez-Melton or Miss Little and watch what they do with themselves.

Golf for The Girls

Good advice is to imagine you are standing on a narrow gauge railway line and have to swing your club so that it runs along the parallel line in front of where your feet are. Who knows, if you go out of bounds on to a railway line this advice might become doubly valuable - provided, of course, that your opponent hasn't spotted that you are out of bounds and provided, also, there is no train coming.

When they are lining up to drive off the tee you may have noticed that many lady golfers first lay their club down on the grass pointing in the direction of the green, then place their toes against the club so that, theoretically, when they swing it will be in the right direction. Where they often go wrong is they then bend down, grunting, to pick up their club and, in so doing, move their feet so that they drive off with massive confidence into the woods at the left. So, if you use this particular ploy, it is suggested that after placing your toes to the club you keep them there and ask someone standing around to pick up your club and hand it to you. Even if this may become a tedious bore to your fellow players, it assures that you keep your feet still.

Once you have hit the ball (assuming you do) don't crumple up like an old paper bag but extend your arms in a wide, beautiful, free arc. One lady golfer I knew always ended every swing by smashing the club shaft on the back of her neck. As a result she spent quite a lot of her spare time in traction but, when on the course, she was an extremely good performer. In this extension of the swing, of course, I must mention again the importance of suitable clothes, of having no tight seams under the armpits, etc.

There are many different kinds of shot to be played in the course of a round of golf, but the swing should remain basically the same. Which is why there is so much blooming talk about it.

14

Hazards
Bunkers

It is the unknown quantity in a bunker shot that defeats lady golfers. We are never sure what may be lurking underneath the sand that might be thrown up when we attack the ball with our sand iron. Somebody's false teeth, mouldy old cheese sandwiches, a Coke bottle or, worse, a large rock which will not only be thrown out but will smash our wrists on impact.

Men, on the other hand, used as they are to having all the nasty things on life's pathway removed in advance by mothers, girl friends, wives and secretaries, step into bunkers with absolute assurance that all is well therein. This is an emotional imbalance that is extremely hard to eradicate and is the fundamental reason why ladies behave rather extraordinarily in bunkers.

The only part-answer to this dilemma is to master the method of getting the ball out, and try hard not to think of what unseen things might be waiting under the sand. It takes the form of getting over first nerves and tackling the thing in the casual careless manner we use when plunging our hands into our wool baskets although knowing that our fingers are frequently pierced deeply by stray darning needles, or whipping open the oven door though knowing on past form that chances are we are going to lose our eyebrows.

The lurking danger we sense in bunkers is increased by the knowledge that it is a MORTAL SIN to even touch one's clubhead to the sand and that the whole thing must be played with blind hope and trust. If women were allowed to burrow around under the ball just for a moment to make sure about rocks, teeth, bottles, etc. our problem would be over and we'd be able to fly the ball out as good if not better than any man alive.

Another psychological problem we have in bunkers is that men tell us that we must hit the sand several inches behind where the ball is lying. None of us honestly believe this.

Intruding Timber.

Another frequent dilemma is when we find ourselves abruptly confronted by a large solid smirking tree. There are three alternatives: we either take a lofted club and sail our ball over the top of it, knowing that this is the stuff dreams are made of and even if we were allowed to discard our clubs and use our bare hands we wouldn't be able to achieve this (watch women throwing balls for dogs); chip out sideways and back on to the elusive fairway, or proceed in a generally forward direction, missing the tree.

If seeking advice from a male golfer you will find he will usually say "play forwards and aim for the tree and this way you'll find you'll sail right past it". Mmm. In actual fact, of course, if you take his advice, this will prove to be the only shot of the game where you actually send the ball where you are aiming, and the next thing you'll be conscious of will be the clanging of ambulance bells as you lie there, surrounded by birds nests, with a throbbing purpling lump on your forehead.

So, all things considered, the best way to deal with this quite frequent phenomenon is to acknowledge the fact that the tree has won, and hack your way back to the fairway with the minimum of strokes.

Getting it Straight.

Line up your shots, we are told, not by observing the distant flag and then bashing away in that general direction, but by selecting something a few feet (yards) away from you that is in direct line with the flag and lining up with that. But a bit of grass in the right position, no matter how charmingly individual it may seem at the time of close and careful selection is, you will find when you momentarily take your eye off it to address the ball, pretty indistinguishable from any other bit of grass to its right or left.

So it is necessary to find a very noticeable sort of thing standing between you and the flag. Something with a strong personality.

A slightly longer piece of grass you might say? But when you address your ball after selecting this long piece of grass you are going to aim for you will find that meanwhile a bewildering quantity of longer pieces of grass have sprung up all around so that you can no more be absolutely sure, cross-your-heart, which was your piece.

Nature never stands still so, unless you happen to have a truly permanent and easily identifiable thing like a bright red stone or somebody's broken spectacle frames laying directly in your line to the flag, this system is fraught with danger.

Carrying a brightly coloured ball point pen and placing it a few feet in front of the ball pointing towards the flag is the best things, but before you do this it would be advisable to check in the Rule Book whether it is allowed. I can't remember seeing Arnold Palmer doing it.

Water Hazards.

It is an acknowledged fact that should there be a tiny pool of water anywhere on the course a lady golfer's ball will find it. Therefore, water hazards either small or of Lock Ness proportions, which are the delight of male course architects, are our most formidable enemy.

Students of elementary psychology have explained this: we don't like to be cold and wet.

Women have to spend so much of their lives bathing babies, washing schoolboys' necks, scrubbing floors, shopping in downpours, fighting with the laundry, defrosting fridges, hosing the garden and sitting between the drenched brushes of the car wash that the merest glimpse of water on a hard-earned day off crumples our self confidence, stifles our brief sense of escape and beckons our warm dry feet waterwards with the inevitability of oncoming wrinkles.

Our male companions, from the safety of the far side, shout across to us to ignore it - to pretend it isn't there. But even knowing that on a good day and with the wind behind us we could easily send a ball further than the width of the hazard, the fact remains: put some water in a hollow and we'll be in it.

The answer? Grudgingly one has to admit that in taking the men's advice lies our only hope of success. Stand there with your eyes glued to your ball. Ignore the happy splash of rising fish and the soughing of water through the troubled reeds. And keep your head down.

Many Clubs provide ball-rescue poles with nets on the end. These nets usually have holes in them just large enough to let a ball through. Or you can buy a private extending pole of your own with a wire basket on the end to carry around in your golf bag. However, even though armed with the most sophisticated equipment, the extraordinary fact remains that although you know there are hundreds of balls for sure lolling about in that water you won't be able to entice a single one out - either your own or anybody else's.

Nobody can explain this: it is a sort of Bermuda Triangle syndrome.

Our Great Strength
Chips (inedible)

If you happen to have a stout tolerant friend, you'll find that getting her to lie on the floor (preferably with her back to you) and chipping over her is a very good way of coming to terms with this shot.

After a few quiet, well-mannered complaints you'll come to realise that the object is to lift the ball off the ground (to avoid the nasty stuff they put around the green) in a little arc, after which it lands on the clean short stuff either to roll unhindered into the hole or glance over its shoulder and double backwards if its gone too far.

Much natural skill is required to achieve this and so it is rather satisfactory and surprising that women are considered, by men, to be quite good at it.

When you are faced with this shot the secret is to be natural. Forget about the ball, the club and the hole. Pretend you are chucking a rejected potato into the kitchen wastebin and use the same wrist action, force and direction. How often have you actually missed with that potato?

With our natural rhythm and bringing into play our deeprooted domestic skills (see above) we should easily more than compensate for the sheer beefy primitive strength that our male opponents have to offer.

So, when their drives land on the edge of the green at a par-four, we should not throw ourselves onto the grass and burst into tears: with our finely developed sense of direction that has led us unerringly over the years to the product we need, hidden though it may be in a maze of supermarket shelves, and our bland potato-throwing skills, we should beat them at what they like to think is their own game.

Golf for The Girls

These days golf courses are not peopled mainly by gentle vicars relaxing from the ardours of delivering yesterday's sermon or retired country gentlemen pottering round whilst idly pondering their next letter to *The Times*, but by highly competitive males who come thundering and blustering towards the first tee like a pride of lions thirsting for blood, so face squarely what you are up against and don't forget your heritage: you are a woman, a member of the thoughtful, considerate and gentle breed. Keep your aggression hidden until you can give full vent to it in the Ladies Change Room, and your tears for crying with laughter as they hook or slice their drives massively out of bounds. Which of course they will do. Quite often.

Utilise the kindly patience you exercise in the home when you spring to fetch his slippers as you hear his key in the door, when you leap to your feet to get his ice from the fridge, when you insist he watches his football even if Jeremy Irons is on the other channel. Lull him into a sense of ridiculously false security so that he doesn't suspect the devious and dedicated plotting of the female mind bent on attaining its object - that neatly wrapped Dunlop 65.

Success and glory to all woman golfers!

In conclusion, a great deal of consideration and body of research into the pitfalls confronting aspiring lady golfers has gone into the compiling of these pages and, if you keep it on your bedside table, committing to memory a new tactic each night before you close your eyes, you will find an ever increasing confidence and purpose when you step, spike footed, towards that first tee.

And a final thought: Never, in the presence of men, say
"It's Only A Game"

The Hangover Handbook & Boozer's Bible
Ever groaned, burped and cursed the morning after, as Vesuvius erupted in your stomach, a bass drummer thumped on your brain and a canary fouled its nest in your throat? Then you need these 100+ hangover remedies. There's an exclusive Hangover Ratings Chart, a Boozer's Calendar, a Hangover Clinic, and you can meet the Great Drunks of History, try the Boozer's Reading Chart, etc., etc.
(In the shape of a beercan) £3.99

The Ancient Art of Farting by Dr. C.Huff
Ever since time began, man (not woman) has farted. Does this ability lie behind many of the so far unexplained mysteries of history? You Bet - because Dr. C.Huff's research shows conclusively there's something rotten about history taught in schools. If you do most of your reading on the throne, then this book is your ideal companion. Sit back and fart yourself silly as you split your sides laughing! *£3.99*

The National Lottery Book: Winning Strategies
An indispensable guide to the hottest lottery systems in the world. Designed to help you find those lucky lottery numbers that could make you rich. ●Learn how to *Play Like the Pros...* ● Discover ways of *Getting an Edge...* ● Improve your chances with the *'Wheeling Technique'...* ● Find possible ways of *Making it Happen* for you... ● See how understanding betting *Psychology and Equitability* can seriously *Improve Your Winnings...* ● Plus lots more *General Tips* to help you win! £4.99

Rude Cats (for cat lovers everywhere)
If you have ever wondered what your average moggie has been up to as it staggers back over the garden wall, covered in scar tissue and licking its rear end, then "RUDE CATS" is for you. Join Randy, an old campaigner on a sexually explicit journey of discovery into the twilight world beyond the cat-flap and prepare to be shocked! £3.99

The Armchair Guide to Football
An inexpensive and humorous look at the state of modern football. Is it really run by money crazed businessmen who don't care about tradition? Will Fantasy Football remove the need for pitches, players and footballs? Only £1.99

The Armchair Guide to Fishing
Just why do people go fishing? Is it the basic hunting instinct or do they just love drowning maggots? Only £1.99

The Armchair Guide to Golf
From the serious handicap hunter to the weekend hacker, everybody involved with golf will appreciate this humorous view from the 'inside'. Only £1.99

MORE GOOD BOOKS...

For Adult Eyes Only

Sexy stereograms that will keep you up all night.! Here is a collection of naughty pictures you'll just stare at... and stare at... and stare at... Hidden in each of the splashes of colour are racy views, suggestive items and daring positions. Honestly, you just won't believe your eyes - and that's even after you've mastered seeing the stereograms!!! Full Colour. Hardback. £6.99

A Good Deed for Every Day

The caring, sharing nineties have emphatically replaced the 'me first' eighties. Everybody is becoming less aggressive and starting to look for ways to be pleasant to their fellow human beings. None of the 365 deeds are a big deal. And that is their beauty. They are small, unpretentious acts which won't draw attention to the performer. Indeed the only reward you will get is the inner knowledge that you have made someone else's life just that little bit more pleasant. £3.99

Sex Trivia: A Bedside Companion

Does sex turn you on? Then there's a bedside companion that's titillating, erotic, bizarre, sizzling, shocking, stupendous, hilarious, oddball, staggering... and packed with thousands of TRUE FACTS (all you've ever wanted to know) about your favourite pastime. Find out about... ❤ Killer Condoms ❤ Boomerang Erections ❤ Orgasm as a painkiller ❤ Male Chastity Belts ❤ Sex-aholics Anonymous.. and more! £3.99.

The Drinking Man's Survival Guide

Discover how to celebrate the joys of drinking... stock up on excuses to get you out of trouble, drink for free... learn to sip and save by making your own beer and wine... make recipes to eat your favourite booze... and meet the world's most amazing drinkers. £3.99